# LET THEM PLAY

BY MARGOT THEIS RAVEN

ILLUSTRATED BY CHRIS ELLISON

Most folks say it was Coach Ben Singleton who pulled the all-star dreams from the sky over Harmon Field and sprinkled them in the eyes of 14 boys the summer of 1955. Not that baseball dreams weren't already rising high as heat waves on noonday porches all over Charleston's Upper Westside.

Boys wanted to be Jackie Robinson playing for the Brooklyn Dodgers, and mothers like Flossie Bailey on Strawberry Lane wanted to find their missing mop handles. Stickball players like her son John used the handles as bats to hit half-rubber balls, and sandlot players made mitts from paper bags or cardboard sewn with shoelaces.

But every street and sandlot player knew the lucky boys suited up for one of the four Little League teams chartered by the Cannon Street YMCA. Those boys used *real* bats, balls, and gloves and wore *real* uniforms. They played on Harmon Field, too, a sun-spit patch of earth where the players rolled out a red picket fence before each game to mark the home run line!

That Jackie Robinson summer, it wasn't just Charleston's Westside boys that loved playing ball. Baseball fever burned all over South Carolina. The state had 62 chartered Little Leagues in all—but only the Cannon Street league was black. All the other leagues were white.

In South Carolina in 1955, no white Little League team ever played a black team, because white people and black people were said to live *separate but equal*. That meant black people had to use separate schools. Separate parks. Separate ball fields, too—even though every chartered Little League team signed a paper to play "any team regardless of race, color, or creed."

But that summer, like blue crabs tucked deep in the mud banks of Charleston's marsh creeks, parents, neighbors, and coaches tried to keep the dark troubles and deep worries of the times from the Westside boys who just wanted to play baseball. And the more baseball the better!

One day, in the small front room where Mr. Robert Morrison, president of the Cannon Street YMCA, made important decisions, Coach Singleton and the other coaches met to pick the first all-black Little League all-star team in South Carolina. Called the Cannon Street All-Stars, the team would compete in the city tournament, and then could advance to the state competition, and then to the regional tournament in Rome, Georgia. If they won there, it was off to the Little League World Series in Williamsport, Pennsylvania!

Coach Singleton hit the exciting idea to the 14 chosen boys like a high pop fly! "Big Maj, can you pitch an extra tournament game?" he grinned. Leroy Major grinned back!

Soon all-star dreams sparkled in Westside parents' eyes: Mothers held teas as fund-raisers to buy uniforms, making heaps of fried chicken, sweet johnnycakes, and bread pudding that melted in your mouth, set out on best linens and good china. Fathers who worked at the Navy Yard went straight to the ball field to help out. Nothing was too good for the boys!

But the dark fears hidden from the boys bubbled to light when the state's Little League director heard that white all-star teams must compete against an all-black team.

He said: No white team would play Cannon Street. Not in Charleston or anywhere! The director withdrew from Little League to start his own boys' baseball program. He encouraged state teams to boycott Little League, too. Like a dream gone nightmare, every white South Carolina Little League joined the new baseball program. The boycott eventually spread through 11 southern states, making Cannon Street the only Little League franchise left in the South, and the All-Stars became the team nobody would play.

Even though the Cannon Street boys were the state winners and Southeastern Champs, they had won by default. They had not played a single game to advance to the Little League World Series. Officials in Williamsport ruled the boys could not compete in the final tournament.

Mid-August on Harmon Field, 14 boys watched Ben Singleton thump a bat on a bench at sundown. Thump, thump, Ben drummed, trying to find the right words. He had seven children of his own, including his son, Maurice, second baseman on the All-Stars team, but he loved every one of these fine boys as if they were his own. He wanted them to stay fine. He knew the man you condemn today is the one you become tomorrow.

"Boys, I've got news," he finally spoke. "Little League has invited us as official guests to the World Series in Williamsport. They say they'll treat you like the other play-off teams. And I promise you'll be met by fire trucks and cheering people," he added.

But he didn't promise the boys that they *would* play.

Still he hoped that when they got to Williamsport, he and the other coaches could persuade Little League President Peter McGovern to let the boys take the field for at least one game.

On the day of the trip, mothers packed clean clothes and new pajamas for the boys
stay in a real college dorm! Flossie Bailey filled a food hamper with johnnycakes
and ham sandwiches for her son John's long bus ride.

That evening, the boys and men—coaches, managers, and YMCA officials—met by a
blue bus at the YMCA. The bus was old and battered, but it seemed like a rocket ship
to Mars to the boys. For most of them it was their first trip out of South Carolina.

At 9 p.m. the bus lumbered down Cannon Street for the 745-mile trip. Windows
down, the boys waved to each parent, sister, brother, relative, and neighbor who'd
come to see them off.

On the road the boys talked so much about the tournament games, they could
almost taste in their mouths the dream to play just like the sweet smells coming
from John Bailey's food hamper. At last the boys nodded off, but not before Leroy
Majors and Vermont Brown tried to pry a sleeping John Bailey's fingers off that
hamper to get at Flossie's johnnycakes!

Just outside of Williamsport, the boys found out that Coach Singleton was a man
of his word. When the bus broke down and suddenly caught on fire, a fire truck
put out the flames. As the repaired bus traveled once more, the boys arrived in
Williamsport just as Mr. Singleton had promised: led by the fire truck down the
steep hill into town.

The boys stayed at Lycoming College where the other eight series teams were also housed. That first night, far too excited to sleep, the boys had a pillow fight in their new pajamas to tamp down lots of feelings. In the morning, the other teams urged the Cannon Street boys to eat breakfast with them.

"Who's your home run hitter?" the other players asked right away. "That would be me, fella!" Allen Jackson smiled back proudly.

After breakfast, Leroy Major gasped, "Look at that!" Through the dining hall windows he saw David Middleton and Maurice Singleton signing autographs for a bevy of girls. The other boys ran outside, too, grinning at signing their names as if they were somebodies here.

Meanwhile, behind closed doors, Ben Singleton and the Cannon Street coaches met with Peter McGovern to ask one last time if the All-Stars could play.

A decision was made. Then dressed in official Little League T-shirts, the Cannon Street team rode the old blue bus to Original Little League Field for the play-off games.

When the boys walked into Carl E. Stotz Stadium, 5,000 spectators clapped for the team they'd read about in newspapers: *the boycotted Negro team from South Carolina*. The crowd kept cheering as the boys took front-row seats of honor behind a red WELCOME banner!

Before the play-off games began, each team took a field warm-up. Suddenly, a loudspeaker announced the Cannon Street All-Stars would take their field warm-up now. The boys leapt to their feet and ran onto that baseball diamond of dreams to finally show what they could do!

The crowd gasped when Allen Jackson rifled the ball from the outfield to home plate as if he really *were* Jackie Robinson. The Cannon Street boys burned up the field. Graceful. Powerful. As the boys threw, people in the stands rose to their feet.

Rose with the hopes of the boys to play. Rose to stomp the bleachers until the whole stadium rocked—and a chant began! A chant from thousands of stomping, clapping, cheering people who demanded over and over again for the boys:

LET THEM PLAY!  LET THEM PLAY!  LET THEM PLAY!

The boys kept throwing as the chant went on and on and the crowd demanded even louder:

LET THEM PLAY!   LET THEM PLAY!

It was a chant that told the 14 players they were on the ball field where they belonged. A chant that said you can't steal a boy's dream to succeed, like a Jackie Robinson slide into home. A chant that said they were *not* the team *nobody* would play.

They were the team that had won a crowd's heart.

Then suddenly, the Cannon Street All-Stars' time, on the greenest, smoothest field they'd ever seen, was over. The boys sat back in their seats, and for the rest of the day watched the games they'd come to play. The warm-up practice was the only field-time Little League could offer.

The Cannon Street boys watched the home run that gave the Morrisville, Pennsylvania team its extra-inning World Series victory. That team went home on a new bus, led by a police motorcycle escort. The All-Stars from South Carolina went home as they had come—on a battered blue bus.

It was a quiet trip home as each boy and coach swallowed down sadness. But as they neared Charleston, Coach Singleton thought how far they had just traveled on an old bus and a new dream to live equal—*everywhere*—not separate—*anywhere*.

"We sure had a time of it, didn't we?" he smiled at young faces that now smiled back.

When the bus pulled up to the YMCA, family and friends were there to greet them. The boys walked home along Cannon Street, and spoke of green grass smooth as glass, a home run wall to sail a ball over, and a chant from 5,000 people they would never, never forget:

### LET THEM PLAY!

## [ Epilogue ]

On August 16, 2002, 14 men boarded a sleek air-conditioned bus in Charleston, South Carolina, headed for the 2002 Little League World Series championship in Williamsport, Pennsylvania. Forty-seven years earlier, they'd made that same trip as 11- and 12-year-old boys.

When the bus arrived in Williamsport for the Opening Ceremonies, memories rolled the summer of 1955 into a leather ball stitched with the red threads of time. As almost 60-year-old men with gray hair, the Cannon Street All-Stars stood on the field before teams from all around the world and were presented the South Carolina State Championship Banner at last. They held the banner together as new crowds shouted and clapped for them.

Norman Robinson,'55 Cannon Street's catcher, borrowed a bat from an eight-year-old Little Leaguer. A pitch came to him. He hit the ball like a cannon shot. It soared over the home run wall as he rounded the bases, high-fived and cried; tears flowing down his face and his teammates' for the boys they once were and the fine men they had become.

The ball soared with their hearts back to a summer when 14 ball players found out all the stars that ever mattered already glistened in the eyes of the people waiting for them:

—the boys they loved—and were so proud of—
to get off a blue bus at the Cannon Street YMCA.

**Coach:**
Benjamin "Sink" Singleton (Head Coach All-Stars)

**Assisting All-Star Coaches:**
Walter Burke, Rufus Dilligard, A.O. Graham,
Lee J. Bennett, R.H. Penn

**Cannon Street YMCA League Teams:**
Fielding Funeral Home; Harleston-Boags Funeral Home;
The Police Athletic League (PALS); Pan-Hellenic Council.

**Cannon Street YMCA President:**
Mr. Robert Morrison

**Charleston American Little League President
and Team Historian:**
Augustus Holt

**The 14 All-Stars Players (nicknames and positions)**
• Power switch-hitter and first baseman, Allen Jackson
• Home run hitting shortstop with hands of glue, John Rivers
• Outstanding cleanup batter and third baseman, Carl "Carly" Johnson

• Strong, steady, hitting catcher, Arthur "Dud" Peoples
• Double-playmaking second baseman, "Little Weaze" Charles Bradley
• Deft left fielder and strong hitter, John Bailey
• Home run smasher, left fielder, William "Buck" Godfrey
• Strong, solid catcher, "'Lil Grey" Vernon Grey
• Booming hardball pitcher and center fielder, "Big Maj" Leroy Major
• Big playmaking first baseman, "Hambaloney" John Mack
• Out-of-the-park-hitter, second baseman, David Middleton
• Hit-the-dirt-to-get-any-ball-back, great defensive catcher, Norman Robinson
• Heads-up second baseman, "'Lil Sink" Maurice Singleton
• Control-pitcher and first baseman, Vermont "Pop" Brown
• Alternates were: Leroy Carter and George Gregory, Strong fielders and hitters

*To the love and memories between fathers and sons—*
*especially Gus and Lawrence Holt.*

—Margot Theis Raven


*In memory of Lawrence Holt.*

—Chris Ellison

**The 1955 Cannon Street All-Stars in the dining hall at Lycoming College. Cannon Street League President Mr. Robert (Bob) Morrison is seated at the center of the table. Mr. Lee Bennett, the only surviving adult member of the 1955 trip, is seated at Mr. Morrison's right.**

Photo used with permission from the Charleston American Little League

**Sleeping Bear Press**™

2395 South Huron Parkway, Ste. 200
Ann Arbor, MI 48104
www.sleepingbearpress.com

Printed and bound in the United States.

15 14 13 12 11 10 9

Library of Congress Cataloging-in-Publication Data

Raven, Margot Theis.

Let them play / written by Margot Theis Raven; illustrated by Chris Ellison.
p. cm.
ISBN 978-1-58536-260-8
1. Little league baseball—South Carolina—Charleston—History—Juvenile literature. 2. Little League World Series (Baseball) (1955)—Juvenile literature. 3. Discrimination in sports—United States—History—Juvenile literature. I. Ellison, Chris, ill. II. Title.
GV880.5.R38 2005
796.352'62—dc22      2004027298